COMPANION GUIDE

SECRET DIARY UNLOCKED
MY STRUGGLE TO LIKE ME

Suzy Weibel

Moody Publishers

CHICAGO

© 2007 by
SUZY WEIBEL

All Scripture quotations, unless otherwise indicated, are taken from the *Holy Bible, New International Version*®. NIV®. Copyright © 1973, 1978, 1984 by International Bible Society. Used by permission of Zondervan. All rights reserved.

Scripture quotations marked TNIV are taken from the *Holy Bible, Today's New International Version*®. TNIV®. Copyright© 2001, 2005 by International Bible Society. Used by permission of Zondervan. All rights reserved.

Editor: Pam Pugh
Book cover/interior design: Julia Ryan / www.DesignByJulia.com
Original cover image: JupiterImages, www.comstock.com
Feathery doodle: Dara Lowry

Library of Congress Cataloging-in-Publication Data

Weibel, Suzy.
  Secret diary unlocked. Companion guide : my struggle to like me /
by Suzy Weibel.
    p. cm.
  Includes bibliographical references.
  ISBN 978-0-8024-8080-4
  1. Teenage girls--Religious life--Study and teaching. 2.
Self-acceptance in adolescence--Study and teaching. 3.
Self-acceptance--Religious aspects--Christianity--Study and
teaching. I. Title.
BV4551.3.W455 2007
248.8'33--dc22

2007008718

ISBN: 0-8024-8080-2
ISBN-13: 978-0-8024-8080-4

We hope you enjoy this book from Moody Publishers. Our goal is to provide high-quality, thought-provoking books and products that connect truth to your real needs and challenges. For more information on other books and products written and produced from a biblical perspective, go to www.moodypublishers.com or write to:

Moody Publishers
820 N. LaSalle Boulevard
Chicago, IL 60610

1 3 5 7 9 10 8 6 4 2

Printed in the United States of America

CONTENTS

LESSON 1

JOURNEY TO THE

JOURNEY TO THE
CENTER OF YOUR WORLD
(AN OVERNIGHT ADVENTURE!)

THE GOAL:

Enjoying a "getting to know you" session that visits both contemporary culture . . . and the ancient world of the group leaders!

THINGS YOU'LL NEED:

- Games from your decade
- DVDs of your favorite old movies (VHS or even Beta!)
- Old music
- Atari or Genesis video games
- A corded wall phone, etc.

GETTING READY:

- Read chapters 1–2 of *Secret Diary Unlocked*
- Preview study guide materials
- Set up/decorate large livable space for a huge retro slumber party (music and DVD capabilities needed)
- Name tag/arrival station
- Leaders need to bring old photos/yearbooks to event

- Leaders create "How I Feel About Me" collages
- Rent an appropriate "time travel" or classic decade movie
- Purchase lots and lots of slumber party treats!

 ## THE PAJAMA PARTY

THE GAME: NAME TAGS

TIME: 20 MINUTES

THE RULES: CREATIVITY

PARTY SUPPLIES: CREATIVE, THEMED TAGS

THE GAME: PHOTO SHARE

TIME: 15 MINUTES

THE RULES: LEADERS ONLY

PARTY SUPPLIES: OLD PHOTOS/YEARBOOKS

THE GAME: FAST GAME OF CHOICE

TIME: 30 MINUTES

THE GAME: COLLAGES

TIME: 50 MINUTES

THE RULES: NO RULES, JUST RIGHT

PARTY SUPPLIES: A LOT OF CREATIVE ART SUPPLIES

THE GAME: TRUTH OR DARE

TIME: 30 MINUTES

THE RULES: LEADERS CHOOSE ALL GAME OPTIONS

PARTY SUPPLIES: NONE

THE GAME: DISCUSSION

TIME: 40 MINUTES
THE RULES: NO STORIES LEAVE THIS ROOM
PARTY SUPPLIES: COPY OF SECRET DIARY UNLOCKED

THE GAME: MOVIE

TIME: 2 HOURS
THE RULES: TIME TRAVEL
PARTY SUPPLIES: SCREEN AND DVD PLAYER

The idea behind this session is that the girls would get to know you as leaders and get a taste of what a slumber party might have been like "back in the day." Choose your theme! A fifties party with hair curlers and Frankie and Annette movies? The seventies, chock-full of black light posters and lava lamps? Or would your girls love a sports-themed night with a lot of active games and a viewing of *A League of Their Own*? Have fun . . . and think outside the box!

THE ARRIVAL

 As the girls arrive, have theme-oriented music playing on an appropriate sound system. How cool would it be to actually be playing records—yes, vinyl—as the girls arrive? Direct the girls to an area where they can custom-make their own name tag for the event. Try to keep name tags in line with the theme of the party; for instance, if your theme is the seventies each of the girls could make a beaded necklace that has her name on it, or let them design their own "pet rock." An eighties name tag could have a Rubik's Cube or Pac Man theme.

THE GREETING

Welcome the girls to the party and take a couple of minutes to introduce the leaders. Have the leaders share a picture of themselves from their middle or high school years as part of their introduction, as well as a story or diary entry from that time of their lives. Tell the girls that tonight is all about girl time, getting to know one another, and a reminder that a girl is a girl is a girl . . . They will soon see that despite any age differences, girls know how to be girls, and you never have to tell a lady how to have fun at a slumber party!

GAME NUMBER ONE

Kick the night off with a rowdy game of some sort. Sardines might be a good option (hide and seek, group style, in the dark) if you are in your church building. Capture the Flag could be fun in good weather. Keep-away in the pool? A big snowball fight? It depends on your girls, your theme, and the weather . . . but make it loud, fast, and fun! Google the phrase "fun group games" if you want a plethora of great ideas!

SESSION ONE: IT WAS A GOOD YEAR

Read chapter 1 of *Secret Diary Unlocked: My Struggle to Like Me* out loud to the girls. Have the girls circle around in their pj's, supply plenty of junk food—or health food if you think it will actually be consumed— in the center of the circle, and invite those stuffed animals to attend too! Choose a leader who enjoys reading and can communicate with a variety of vocal inflections to do this reading. You'll want to be sure the girls are fully engaged. *Though girls often enjoy the opportunity to read aloud, they tend to process information better if an experienced reader is covering the material. If you want to include the girls, allow them to take turns reading the diary entries included in each chapter.*

Allow girls a few minutes to complete the "My Struggle" journal entry at the end of the chapter. For larger groups, this session may be done in smaller groups of twenty girls or less.

Provide the girls with a huge supply of various art mediums—paper, magazines, digital camera and printer, stickers, stamps, confetti of various sorts, noodles, ribbon, feathers, etc. Ask them to create an abstract art piece that reflects how they feel about themselves—physically, spiritually, socially, in their family, tonight specifically . . . Show them your own artwork (prepared in advance) and explain some of the choices you made. You know, of course, the more vulnerable and transparent you are willing to be, the more the girls will feel free to be the same.

GAME NUMBER TWO

Play the most famous slumber party game of all . . . Truth or Dare! Use the list found in appendix A or create your own, but be sure all questions and dares will be pleasing to God first and foremost. This is a game that needs to be redeemed for many of these girls, and you probably need to ask the girls if they have ever played a game of Truth or Dare that they have regretted.

** *There is a Web site called www.tordol.com that allows you to play a G-rated game of Truth or Dare. It may be a bit less personal than the appendix questions, but is easy and fun to use. The G rating is truly* *appropriate, and there are over 9,500 questions, some of which I have borrowed for this section.*

SESSION TWO: COLLIDING WORLDS

Go over the *My Struggle* session on page 28 of *Secret Diary Unlocked*. Try to keep this time light and fun, keeping stories from your own past short and allowing the girls to have fun with your "old-fashionedness." They will love it. If you can, bring a few pictures along—pictures of yourself when younger (the more embarrassing and dated, the better), pictures made famous by a magazine such as *Life* during your teen years, and perhaps a few pictures of the big heartthrobs of your day. Bring in a high school yearbook or two and allow the girls to flip through these. And trust me, you don't need to be afraid to let them read the things written by classmates on the autograph pages. One of the best things I ever did for a student who was rebellious and making some big decisions about what direction her crowd would be taking her was to give her my diary, a bowl of popcorn, a big pillow, and a warm blanket and send her into my walk-in closet to read for a couple of hours. I was a mess back in '79! And yet her response was, "Oh my gosh . . . you were just like me." She told me later that it was on that day she decided to trust me with her life.

After 20 minutes or so of stories and laughing, look together at the *Your World* section of chapter 2 together. Use the following questions for discussion, but before you begin, remind the girls of the importance of this cardinal rule: What is said in this room stays in this room. There will be no sharing of someone else's story after tonight!

QUESTIONS FOR DISCUSSION:

● What kind of impact do the statistics in this chapter have on you? Do you feel scared? Astonished? Like "it won't happen to me"?

● How aware do you think your parents are of the things you see and hear daily?

● What aspect of a teenager's daily life, in your opinion, places her in the most danger?

● How would you feel if parents became more technologically savvy? (It would undoubtedly ruin some of your friends!) Would you like parents to take more interest in what is on your computer screen, what you are listening to, and what movie you've just been to see?

READ THROUGH 2 TIMOTHY 3:1-5 AND THEN INSTRUCT THE GIRLS AS FOLLOWS:

I am going to read these verses again, and I want you to close your eyes and get a picture in your mind. There is a room in which you have gathered all of your friends— those with whom you hang out on a regular basis. It's a party room and your friends are free in this room to do whatever they please, whether good or bad. Take note of what your friends are doing as I read through these verses.

READ 2 TIMOTHY 3:1-5 AND ALSO VERSE 9 THIS TIME.

Ask: **What were your friends doing?** *(Allow girls to respond either verbally or by what will inevitably happen—they will look at one another and giggle. Verbal chaos may even ensue for a moment!)*

<u>Tell the girls:</u> **A lot of you may have just seen your friends in obvious folly. While it may be best to separate from a friend or two whom you just observed in your mind, there is another action step you can take to avoid being a statistic. During the course of this Bible study we are going to deal with self more than with others. Back in the eighties this was kind of a taboo thing to say in the church, but we're beginning to see again that it is pretty important: We need to love ourselves. We need to know that we are loved by God, that though we have done nothing to deserve it He values us, that our lives have a purpose, and that He is madly jealous for our love. If all of the girls in your "party room" truly knew all of that, do you think it might have an impact on their choices? Do you think it might keep them safer? I think so. His love and our obedience to the One who loves us is the greatest shield we have ever had, way back in my world, and here in your world today.**

Close this session by praying for the girls, that they would in the course of this study come to see how deeply and passionately they are loved by God the Father.

MOVIE TIME

After a 20-minute snack and chat break, call the girls back into a common area and play a fun "back in time" movie to end the evening. There are a lot of time-travel movies out there—your local video store clerk should be able to help you.

LESSON 2

BOY CRAZY!

THE GOAL:

To help the girls plan a healthy balance in their lives

THINGS YOU'LL NEED:

- 3 x 5 note cards
- 4 stuffed animals
- One object covered in "fur" or soft cloth
- One metallic object
- Set of balances or two small scales
- Marbles or landscaping rock
- Science lab coat *(** See below)*

GETTING READY:

- Read chapter 3 of *Secret Diary Unlocked*
- Preview study guide materials
- Create name tags for opening game

**Extra fun: Create a portion of the room to be a "mad scientist's laboratory"

THE GAME: WHO AM I?

TIME: 10 MINUTES
THE RULES: GUESS WHOSE NAME IS ON BACK
PARTY SUPPLIES: NOTE CARDS

THE GAME: BOYS, BOYS, BOYS

TIME: 30 MINUTES
THE RULES: GIRL TALK—WHO IS ON THE THRONE?
PARTY SUPPLIES: STUFFED ANIMALS AND OBJECTS

THE GAME: SCALE CHALLENGE

TIME: 20 MINUTES
THE RULES: LAB SESSION—HOW ARE YOUR SCALES?
PARTY SUPPLIES: SCALES; ROCKS OR MARBLES

THE GAME: THRONE INVITATION

TIME: 10 MINUTES
THE RULES: SMALL GROUP PRAYER
PARTY SUPPLIES: NONE

Girls like boys and boys like girls. As much as I often want to discourage this as a parent, I know in the long run I'm not going to make much headway! The attraction is indeed natural. I've recently been walking through a situation with a friend where her daughter was given a little too much freedom a little too soon. The freedom we give to our girls is not a bad thing. It is a necessary part of separation to begin to hand over more control. At this age, however, girls really need moms, mentors, and trustworthy peers to help them keep things in balance. This session will give your girls a chance to set the scales to "balance" where boys are concerned.

WHO AM I?

As the girls arrive, place a name card on each girl's back, but do not allow her to see the name as you do so. Each of these cards should have printed on it the name of a guy that girls may consider teen "idols"—maybe Zac Efron, Chad Michael Murray, Leonardo DiCaprio, etc. The girls may then mill about the room asking each other ONLY yes-or-no questions for 5 minutes or so. After a time, ask the girls to line up and guess whose name was on their back.

SESSION: THE THRONE

Have the girls take turns reading Suzy's diary entries and the responses from other girls aloud. <u>Ask the girls:</u> **Why do you think this chapter has been subtitled "Looking for Attention"?**

Suzy mentions in this chapter that the number one need for humans is to know that they are loved. Love is a powerful force in a person's life. One of the first studies done on the impact of love was by a University of Wisconsin scientist, Harry Harlow, in the 1950s. Harlow completed three study phases using newborn rhesus monkeys. *(Use various stuffed animals to give the girls a visual for this.)* **Harlow first separated the newborn monkeys from their mothers and placed them in a cage with two substitute "mothers." The first substitute was a "monkey" covered with furry cloth, but it offered no form of nourishment.** *(Place a stuffed "monkey" next to the inanimate object you have covered with something furry.)* **In the same cage was a wire mother that had no fur whatsoever. Though this wire monkey "provided"**

nourishment for the baby in the form of milk in a baby bottle, she could not play, cuddle, or provide warmth for the infant. *(Place a second stuffed "monkey" next to a metallic inanimate object.)* Harlow's first observation was that the newborn monkeys visited the wire "mother" only for milk. The rest of their waking and sleeping hours were with the fur-covered "mother," where they could cuddle and sleep. *(Move the stuffed "infant" from the wire covered object to the side of the fur-covered one.)*

Next, Harlow separated the monkeys into two groups. One group was constantly with a fur-covered "mother" that was equipped with a bottle of milk, and the second group was constantly with the wire "mother," who still had her bottle of nourishment to offer. The young monkeys were no longer able to move back and forth between the two "mothers." *(Separate the stuffed "infants," placing one with your fur-covered object and one with your wire-covered object.)*

The results of the study were terribly sad. *(Refer once again to your stuffed animal models as you go along.)* The monkeys who had been with the fur mothers were well socialized, playful, and content and turned into fine mothers themselves. The monkeys in the second group, however, showed signs of emotional disturbance, choosing not to seek comfort from their wire "mother" when frightened or threatened, but instead throwing themselves upon the floor, clutching their knees, and rocking back and forth. *(Isolate this "infant" from the other, cloth-raised "infant".)* These monkeys were frequently unable to mate, and were completely uninterested in their own infants when they did give birth. Rhesus infants who had been separated from all mothering influences (given only a bottle and no substitute "mother" in any form) experienced emotional damage that Harlow and his team declared to be "irreparable." [1]

How does this relate to us then? Most of us are not wire monkey babies! We have been loved and know how to give love, and as a matter of fact, we have been programmed to do so. That longing you have for romance and the perfect wedding, and the happily-ever-after . . . it is very much a result of all the cuddling and nourishment you received when you were young. To keep the monkey analogy going—you're looking for the guy who will sit for hours and pick those fleas out of your fur, aren't you?

Well, he's probably out there all right. But are you ready to meet him? There is a saying that you may have heard . . . you have to put the horse before the cart. Part of the problem with boy craziness—any kind of craziness, for that matter—is that it puts the cart in front of the horse. This is because "craziness" consumes our thoughts. The boy fanatic thinks only about boys. The sports fanatic thinks only about sports. The money fanatic thinks only about gaining wealth. And that is cart-then-horse thinking!

Things have to be done in the proper order if we wish to achieve maximum impact or value. What if the publishers had tried to make all the sales of this book before it had been written? Would they have sold any? *(Girls should recognize that, yes, some would be sold.)* Would it have been the best marketing strategy? Or what if a teacher were to test you before the unit began? Would you and your parents contest your grades? Would you have a right to? Yes!

God has an order for your romance adventure too. He knows, because He created us, that we are prone to worship. Sometimes we're tempted to think that worship is a matter of song and dance, but a better way to look at worship is to ask, "What do I give the most worth to?" Think of it this way. The circle we are sitting in is your heart. This chair *(place a chair in the center of the circle)* is the throne of your heart. There is room on this chair for one. There is only one to whom you can give primary worship, or worth-ship, to. And that is the one on whom you will spend most of your time and energy.

HAVE ONE OF THE GIRLS READ MATTHEW 6:31–34.

<u>Say</u>: I know how much time girls spend worrying about boys. Do I look good enough to be looked at? Will I ever have a boyfriend? Will I ever get married? Will my marriage last? And yet God says that's backwards thinking. "Think about Me first," He says. "Think about how I love you and how I've created you. Think about this world that I've made and how much I love the people in it. Think about how I feed you and clothe you and take care of your every need . . . Don't you think I have that other stuff under control, too?" But it will be very much out of control if He's not in this chair. *(Refer to the "throne.")*

LAB: CHECKING YOUR SCALES

 Have the girls gather around you in your "mad scientist's laboratory." Now is the time to put on your lab coat if you're going all out for this one. (If you have access and want to have fun, have some colored water boiling on Bunsen burners and maybe set a couple pieces of dry ice under the counter.) Show the girls the scales you have brought or the balance if you managed to get ahold of one . . . the balance would actually be the better visual aid. The balance or the scales should clearly be labeled so that all girls can see, one side reading "JESUS" and the other side

reading "THE BOY." Ask for two volunteers. Volunteers need to either have a boyfriend or a serious crush. Only one volunteer will participate at a time, answering the following questions. They will answer questions by placing a rock or a marble on the appropriate side of the scales. Let the girls know in advance that their friends have the right to override their answers, thereby forcing a change in marble/rock placement!

LAB QUESTIONS—VOLUNTEER ONE

- *Which did you think of first today, Jesus or your boy?*
- *Whose name is written all over your notebooks?*
- *Have you ever gone to a new youth group because he was there? Y=b*
- *Do you have a song you've named "your song"? Y=b*
- *Have you cancelled something with friends to hang with him? Y=b*
- *Does he know Jesus? Y=J*
- *Do you talk to him nonstop at night? Y=b*
- *Has your relationship/crush caused you to hurt someone else? Y=b*
- *Do you daydream about him during church or worship? Y=b*
- *Do you sometimes feel desperate when you think about him? Y=b*

LAB QUESTIONS—VOLUNTEER TWO

- *Who did you talk to or about late last night, Jesus or your boy?*
- *Have you ever skipped youth group because he wouldn't be there? Y=b*
- *Have your parents met this guy? Y=J*
- *Are your friends sick of hearing about it? Y=b*
- *Is he where you are or ahead of you spiritually? Y=J*

- *Do you cry a lot as a result of this crush/relationship? Y=b*

- *Are your parents complaining they never see you? Y=b*

- *Have you lied about or for this guy? Y=b*

- *Do you feel a lot of anxiety about losing him or not getting him? Y=b*

- *Do you tend to assess yourself in the mirror based on what he will likely think? Y=b*

THRONE INVITATION

 Divide the group into small groups of no more than five and assign a leader/mentor to each group. Ask each member of the group to quickly report what their scales would have looked like had they been one of the lab volunteers.

Allow the group ten minutes to complete page 44 of *Secret Diary Unlocked*: "Who Is on the Throne?" Close by asking girls to pray (preferably aloud, but silently if they feel they can't pray aloud), inviting Jesus to claim His rightful place on the throne of their heart.

Mentors should ask group members if there are any steps they think they need to take to set their life back in balance at this point. Ask, too, if there is any way you can help—even if it's only as a cheerleader!

LESSON 3

MY PEEPS

THE GOAL:

Girls will be asked to choose their friends' needs above their own.

THINGS YOU'LL NEED:

- Copies of "Letter from Suzy" for each girl (appendix B)
- Pens/pencils
- Stamps
- Blank note cards and envelopes

GETTING READY:

- Read chapter 4 of *Secret Diary Unlocked*
- Preview study guide materials
- Prepare to share story of jealousy/envy
- Arrange for stationery needs

THE GAME: SLAPPING GAME

TIME: 15 MINUTES
THE RULES: KNOW WHICH HAND BELONGS TO YOU!
PARTY SUPPLIES: NONE

THE GAME: GETTING RID OF ENVY

TIME: 35 MINUTES
THE RULES: BABY STEPPIN' TO GOOD FRIENDSHIPS
PARTY SUPPLIES: "A LETTER FROM SUZY"; PENS

THE GAME: "I'M PROUD OF YOU" NOTE CARDS

TIME: 10 MINUTES
THE RULES: WRITE YOUR GOOD FRIEND A LETTER
PARTY SUPPLIES: NOTE CARDS; STAMPS; PENS

Girl world is in some serious trouble. A significant majority of our teenage girls far prefer the company of their male peers to their female peers. This was not always the case. While I am not sure exactly why the shift is occurring, there are a number of things contributing to girl-on-girl meanness, not the least of which are the anonymity of text messaging, instant messaging, and other technical social networking services. ABC's *Primetime with Diane Sawyer* did a special in 2006 on teenage girls and their inexplicable willingness to hurt one another with words. We have yet to talk about mean girls . . . but sometimes best friends are all too willing to hurt one another as well. This study will give girls some tools for encouraging friends not only when they struggle, but also as they succeed.

THE SLAPPING GAME

Instruct the girls to form a circle and then lie down on their tummies (sort of like a collapsed push-up position). Each girl should have her hands in front of her, palms down on the floor. The next step is then for girls to place each hand on the *other side* of the girl lying next to her. Now there are two hands in front of each girl on the floor, though the hands *nearest* each girl belong to her neighbor and not to herself.

The girls will now take turns slapping their hands on the floor with the slapping pattern traveling in a circle. The "starter" will slap her right hand one time if she wishes for the pattern to travel counterclockwise. If the "starter" slaps her left hand two times, the circle of slaps will travel clockwise. The trick, of course, is that perception is thrown off pretty badly—the hand each girl sees next to her head not being her own!

If a girl misses her turn, or if she slaps out of turn, that hand must come out of the circle. This means each girl must mess up twice to be kicked out of the game. The game is over when only one person is left.

SESSION: GETTING RID OF ENVY

Have the girls take turns reading Suzy's diary entries and responses from other girls aloud. <u>Ask the girls:</u> **What does it feel like when you discover that a group of girls, even if you don't like them, don't accept you for who you are?**

On a scale of 1 to 10, how important would you say friendships are to you right now? *(Most girls will rank this up near the 10 mark.)*

There are certain answers to questions that we might call "Sunday school answers." These are answers that you give because you know they are biblical and you know they are expected . . . but they may not necessarily be the truest answer possible. A funny example might be that of the kindergarten teacher who asked her class, "Now class, what is brown and furry and collects nuts for the winter?" Little Johnny was very confused, knowing what was expected of him at church, and so he answered, "It sure sounds like a squirrel, but . . . is it Jesus?" I suppose it's safe to assume you've all given such an answer to me or to another leader in the past.

But sometimes our answers have to be honest, because otherwise research would make us out to be a liar! For instance, in a March 2006 poll (the Barna Group) 84 percent of all teenagers surveyed indicated that friendships were one of their top priorities. Here's a staggering difference for you! Only 1 percent of adults listed friendships as a priority.[1] Is it any wonder that your parents may struggle a bit to understand the importance they see you placing on IM chats or phone calls? The "Sunday school answer" to the question, what would you say is the most important thing in your life? might find you responding, "It sure sounds like my friends, but . . . is it Jesus?" And in this session . . . we're actually going to support your need for those friends!

There is no question that Jesus needs to be first in your life (remember the throne?) to keep things in balance, but in this session we want to focus on your friends and the way in which you need and relate to one another.

Why do you think at this particular time in your life friendships are so important and in the adult years they will be so much less so? *(Allow girls some time to throw out some varied answers. Do not correct any answers, but allow freedom to express thought here.)*

This is where a new trend is coming into play for girls today . . . About the same number of girls who say friendship is important to them (84 percent) will also say that friendship with the opposite sex is preferred to same-gender friendships. We read some of the reasons earlier in this session. Girls fight. They hold grudges. And this one seems to be the biggie—we can't seem to be friends without becoming a threat to one another! Listen to Suzy's breakdown of these jealousies from chapter 4:

- Kim is my friend. Dan likes Kim, but I like Dan. Kim becomes a threat. I no longer like Kim.

- Kim ignores me and makes me feel bad. I get Ginny to ignore Kim with me. Now Kim is the odd girl out. She gets a funny look on her face.

- My teammate Beth is a good ballplayer. Good ball-players get all of the attention. I want attention. I am mad at Beth.

- Steph invites me to her house. Beth doesn't want me to go. Beth doesn't want competition for my attention. Beth is mad at both Steph and me.

I'm just curious to see a show of hands—how many of you have struggled with some of these scenarios? *(You should expect a high percentage. Read them a second time, slowly if necessary.)* The question we then remain with is, why?

Why do girls in particular have such a difficult time holding together what should be one of the most important relationships at this time in their life? *(Give the girls appendix B: A Letter from Suzy)*

(Have girls fill in the blanks as you move through the rest of this section.) **Is everyone ready to begin filling in the blanks? Here we go. The first step is, "Think about OTHERS before I think about ME."** *(Read aloud from chapter 4 of* Secret Diary Unlocked, *Philippians 2:4 and the section below it.)* **Our task now is, as a group, to find a way to turn this information into a baby step that we will take this week. Look where your paper says, "This week I will _____." What would you girls like to commit to doing this week that will let someone else's needs come in front of your own? This may be a thought process that needs to change for you, or it could be something you actually do . . .** *(Allow girls some time to talk and process their ideas. There does not need to be one uniform answer for all girls. Give them plenty of room for individuality.)*

Are we ready for step two? The second step is, "Tell someone you TRUST that you are struggling with jealousy." I know that jealousy has quite a negative connotation—we are not supposed to be envious of one another. But do you know what? Quite frankly . . . if most people were honest . . . jealousy is a BIG struggle! *(Share with the girls a time that you felt envious of someone. Be sure you choose a struggle where you can also share the victory part of the story—do not share a current struggle that has yet to be resolved, unless you know for sure that you are on the upswing. It's important the girls see us practicing these steps in our lives as well, and a little vulnerability never hurt anyone!)*

Be sure to fill in the second blank as well. **Who are you going to talk to this week about your struggles with envy?** *(Assist the girls who are having a difficult time pinning down any envy in their lives by asking some helpful questions. It's a wonderful thought—perhaps there are a few girls out there who truly do not have to wrestle with jealous thoughts.)*

Okay, last baby step. Are you ready to move on? Baby step three is, "Do a RANDOM ACT of KINDNESS for someone you ADMIRE today." Sometimes we get the idea that the people we envy have it a lot better than we do. We convince ourselves that they have no struggles, no disappointments . . . no days when they feel jealous of someone else. Listen to this. *(Read aloud from chapter 4 of* Secret Diary Unlocked, *Matthew 20:28 and the section below it.)* So what do you think? What will you do for baby step three this week? Fill in that last blank—think big, but don't promise yourself the impossible. It's important that when you come back next week you know that you were *able* to complete all three steps, whether you actually do it or not.

LAB: I'M PROUD OF YOU

 You've heard of thank-you notes? Those quaint letters that were written once upon a time to let people know you appreciated their thoughtfulness? At this time the girls will write "I'm Proud of You" notes, or a note of encouragement to a friend. It might be nice to bring a few stamps in case a few girls would like (or need) to mail these rather than hand-deliver them.

Girls, to end tonight I am going to give you a note card and envelope and you are going to write a letter to a friend. We'll call these "I'm Proud of You" notes. Try to think of a good friend who has experienced success lately. Pray before writing, and then go at it! Let her know that you think she is talented and beautiful and that you are very excited about the good things that have been coming her way. Let her know you are there to support her in good times and bad, and it's definitely your pleasure today to be writing a card to her because of good times. Sign your name, seal up the envelope, and pray again. Ask God to give you the strength to remain happy for and supportive of your friend, even if your life doesn't seem as sunny as your friend's. Because there'll come a day you'll want to know she's proud of you!

LESSON 4

LEARNING TO LIKE ME

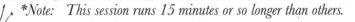

Note: This session runs 15 minutes or so longer than others.

THE GOAL:

~~Girls will recognize (and verbalize) that~~
God is tickled silly pink, madly in love
with them.

THINGS YOU'LL NEED:

- Lyrics for worship songs

- Worship leader

- Name tags

- Copy of *Shallow Hal* with Jack Black

- Scissors

GETTING READY:

- Read chapter 5 of *Secret Diary Unlocked*

- Preview study guide materials

- Arrange for volunteers—stylists and one girl from group

- Rent or buy DVD

- Gather other supplies

THE GAME: WORSHIP

Time: 15 minutes
The Rules: Sing songs of God's creation
Party Supplies: Worship leader; lyrics for girls

THE GAME: YOU'RE BEAUTIFUL

Time: 30 minutes
The Rules: Outer beauty—the world's view
Party Supplies: Makeup artist and stylist; name tags

THE GAME: HOLLYWOOD AGREES!

Time: 15 minutes
The Rules: Inner beauty—God's view
Party Supplies: Shallow Hal clip

THE GAME: NAME EXCHANGE

Time: 10 minutes
The Rules: Putting on the truth
Party Supplies: Name tags; Sharpies; scissors

This may be the biggie for your girls. If there is any one theme that every woman shares, it is the struggle to believe on a daily basis that we are beautiful. Beauty truly is in the eye of the beholder. Often we think this means that I can look at one person and find him attractive and you might look at the same person and say, "Really? Ugh." In a greater sense, however, this beauty maxim applies to our own self. Girls who are not classic beauties can determine they are indeed wonderfully made and walk with a joy and assurance day in and day out, while girls who could by looks alone compete for a spot on the Dallas Cowboys Cheerleader squad wear a mantle of despair and self-loathing underneath their perfect skin. There is no escape for a woman—at some point she has to come to terms with accepting the world's definition of beauty—or the definition of the One who created all that is beautiful.

WORSHIP

I love worship, meaning in this case worship music. Music is a powerful force in kids' lives, and though they may tell you with their secular music that they don't listen to the lyrics, we all know what a smoke screen that is! When put together, lyrics and music have the ability to literally change the human heartbeat. And there is no greater joy for me than watching a student enter fully into God's presence and surrender that heartbeat to Him.

This does not need to be a full band worship experience, though if that scenario is available to you, feel free to change this session time to 30 minutes or more. A guitar and a vocalist will suffice. Simply spend some time singing songs of God's creation and songs of closeness to God. You know what your girls are familiar with, so stick with what moves your particular group. Celebratory songs are fine, too. I can jump with David Crowder for hours and feel that I've just had the ultimate intimate encounter with Jesus.

SESSION: YOU'RE BEAUTIFUL

 Before you begin this session, make arrangements in advance for a surprise guest to attend this meeting. Invite someone who either works in the cosmetic field with make-up, or a woman from the church whom you know to be quite adept in the application of beautiful makeup. Not a painter, if you know what I mean, but someone who can make an "empty" face look amazing with a little bit of color. Choose a girl volunteer, as well. Ask her to come to group with an "empty" face—no makeup at all. You may dismiss her to have her makeup done at this time. Do not tell the rest of the group what she is doing.

If you want to go all-out, you may want to invite a stylist as well, either to cut a new style or simply to do a one-time straighten or curl. You may even choose to outfit your volunteer in some really cool new clothes. It's up to you how crazy you want to get!

Have the girls take turns reading Suzy's diary entries and responses from other girls aloud. <u>Ask the girls:</u> **What makes you feel beautiful?**

Give the girls a small stack of magazines to flip through—*Seventeen*, *Teen Vogue*, *People*, etc. Ask the girls to identify any pictures of girls who look surprisingly "normal." Can they find any girls who look as though they may live next door? Girls whose photos have not been airbrushed? Now look together at a couple of airbrushed photos.

What kinds of feelings do these photos of beauty usually bring up in you?

Why do fashion magazines make so many people feel bad?

Distribute name tags and have the girls put on the name tag, rather than their name, a word that would describe how they have felt about themselves lately. It should be a negative—something they've been struggling with. You can lead the way—if I were to wear one it might say "Lazy" or "Embarrassing" or "Messy." The girls might choose things like "Stupid," "Fat," or "Ugly." Don't worry—these will be exchanged for the truth later on!

Let's go over a few things from the book. I know you were all aware that the fashion industry fixes photos, but we never hear about the times they get in trouble for it, do we? *(Read together pages 78 [One of my favorite stories about retouching] through 79 [What does that say about ME?] from* Secret Diary Unlocked.*)*

What does that say about me? What it needs to say is, "Hey! I guess I could be a movie star! Those girls are just like me! They've taken a normal, everyday girl and made her look that way." Why, instead, do we say, "If someone that beautiful needs to be touched up, then there's no hope for me"?

There is a definition of beauty this world has given us that is completely an outward thing—and it can be achieved by nearly everyone given enough time, money, and skillful artists. The trouble with hanging our mirror on this definition of beauty is that it only affirms us when someone is looking or when we are actually made-up. Eventually, every "beautiful" person has to spend time alone, out of the spotlight, and come face-to-face with the real person inside. And sometimes when we are alone and we see our truest reflection—well, there's not enough makeup in the world to cover that. Beauty should never be mistaken for any kind of remedy for happiness.

Does that mean that beauty in itself is bad or to be avoided? No way! God created this world, and when He saw all that He had made He said it was good. The word *beauty* or *beautiful* appears in the Bible over seventy-five times! In Ecclesiastes it says He makes everything beautiful in its time . . . and then it goes on to explain that we just can't comprehend that. Beauty is God's idea. It pleases Him and He has created us to appreciate beauty as well. Earlier we sent _____ out of the room for a little makeover. Are you ready to see her???? *(Get the girls pumped up!)*

Take some time to ooh and ahh over your volunteer. Ask your makeup artist and stylist to talk a bit about what they have done—and your wardrobe mistress if you chose to do something with clothes. <u>Say:</u> **Okay, so we're good with beauty, but it's all been the world's definition up to now. It's all been outward. There's a Jack Black movie from a while back where Shallow Hal learns a lesson about judging a book by its cover.**

HOLLYWOOD AGREES!

Show clip from *Shallow Hal.*

So what exactly is true beauty? Shallow Hal learned that beauty is reflected from the inside; it isn't fairly represented by the outside. Is that biblical? Let's check out a couple of verses.

(Read 1 Peter 3:3.) **Does this line up with the idea that true beauty is first of all inward?**

(Read Proverbs 31:30–31.) **How does this fit with the same idea?**

But the main thing you girls need to hear comes straight from God's heart in Psalm 139. Why don't you girls get comfy right now—lie back and relax. Close your eyes. Put your head down. I want you to hear this straight from God to you. *"For you created my inmost being; you knit me together in my mother's womb. I praise you because I am fearfully and wonderfully made; your works are wonderful, I know that full well. My frame was not hidden from you when I was made in the secret place. When I was woven together in the depths of the earth, your eyes saw my unformed body. All the days ordained for me were written in your book before one of them came to be. How precious to me are your thoughts, O God! How vast is the sum of them! Were I to count them, they would outnumber the grains of sand. When I awake, I am still with you"* (Psalm 139:13–18).

Keep your eyes closed.

Girls, do you understand? Do you understand that God is tickled silly pink, madly in love with you? He thinks about you all the time. No one on earth can do that, but God can. Do you understand that when He created the earth—thousands of years ago— that He had already on that day ordained for you every one of your days? He knit you together, not some impersonal science called biology. He breathed life into you, and He has stayed with you every day since.

I want you to repeat this after me: God . . . Is . . . Tickled . . . Silly . . . Pink . . . Madly . . . In . . . Love . . . With . . . Me!!!!! Say it again! God is tickled silly pink . . . madly in love with me!!!! One last time: God is tickled silly pink, madly in love with me!

LAB: NAME EXCHANGE

Girls, to end this lesson I'm going to give you a SECOND name tag. I think you know that the name you are wearing right now is NOT a name that God has given to you! God has another name for you, and what we are going to do right now is ask God what that new name should be. We'll take some time to pray, and when you feel confident that you know what name God wants to give you that is TRUTH, you take off the old name and put on the new one. Then I want you to take that old name tag over to the garbage can where there are scissors waiting for you . . . and I want you to cut it into about a million pieces!!! We leave here tonight, ladies, wearing the truth. God is tickled silly pink, madly in love with YOU! Let's pray . . .

LESSON 5

MEAN GIRLS

THE GOAL:

Girls will choose what they will use their tongues for—to praise God or to curse man. Understood—both cannot happen at once.

THINGS YOU'LL NEED:

- Copies of character sketches for volunteers
- Pens/pencils

GETTING READY:

- Read chapter 6 of *Secret Diary Unlocked*
- Preview study guide materials

THE DEAL: TWO TRUTHS AND A LIE

TIME: 20 MINUTES
THE POINT: INTRODUCE "THE LIE"
SUPPLIES: NONE

THE GAME: FOUR TYPES

TIME: 25 MINUTES
THE POINT: CHARACTER SKETCHES OF THREE TYPES
SUPPLIES: THREE VOLUNTEER GIRLS READ SCRIPTS

THE DEAL: CHOOSE A SIDE

TIME: 10 MINUTES
THE POINT: WHICH OF THE FOUR TYPES ARE YOU?
SUPPLIES: NONE

THE DEAL: REVOLUTION

TIME: 10 MINUTES
THE POINT: BEGIN TO MOVE ON TO A BETTER PLACE
SUPPLIES: MY STRUGGLE SECTION FROM CHAPTER 6

Your girls will know all about mean girls before you even begin
this session. Girls being mean to one another is epidemic in our
country right now, to the tune of depression, physical illness, and
even suicide for the victims. Most girls have been a little mean at
one time or another. Most have probably stood by quietly while
someone else was being hurt. But I'd be willing to bet that 100
percent of them have been on the receiving end of meanness.
It hurts. The main goal of this session is to get the girls into three

camps, all of which have the same big goal in the end—whether they are mean, a target, or comfortable where they are, their tongues are to be used for praising God and building one another up. Period. No other options.

TWO TRUTHS AND A LIE

This is a well-known game—perhaps you've played it before—but it will introduce the concept of LIES to the girls in a fun way.

You will go first so the girls get the hang of this, but each person who participates (there may not be time for ALL girls to participate up front) will tell the group three things about themselves. Two things will be true, and one thing will be a lie—a little white lie. Okay, maybe a big, fat lie. The trick to being successful with this game is to choose truths that don't seem like you and a lie that seems like you. For instance, when I play I often say, "I was the first girl in Fort Wayne to play Little League baseball. I once won a beauty pageant. I played tackle football up until sixth grade." The first two are true. I did play baseball and I did (at age 5) win a pageant. Most people believe the pageant is false . . . I haven't worn a dress in years and I never wear makeup. The third is often believed to be true because I am still a competitive athlete.

SESSION: FOUR TYPES

Before you begin this session, you will need to prepare three girls in advance to help you as volunteers. You can either give them their script when they arrive at group or you can give them the script early so they can practice and maybe even come "in costume." You may also choose to use college interns or something of that sort to play these roles . . . It really depends what is available to you.

Girls, I'm going to introduce some friends tonight who are going to share their story with you. I want you to listen to them carefully. After they share, as a matter of fact, I'm going to have you choose which one you identify with most closely. One thing ties these girls together quite closely. Lies. That's right. There are lies being told, and lies being believed. Only after *one* of the girls decides to confront the lies head-on will we see any sign of God's love penetrating this mess of a situation! First, I would like to introduce Mean Eileen!

(Mean Eileen is found in appendix C.)

LEADER: **Thank you, Eileen. That was really brave of you to say those things. Next I want you to meet my friend Sidekick Sally . . .**

(Sidekick Sally is found in appendix D.)

LEADER: **Thank you, Sally.** *(To the big group)* **This is getting complicated, isn't it? I don't know if you've found yet who you identify with, but I still have a couple of friends to introduce you to, so hang in there. Next I'd like you to meet Poor Polly. Thank you for being willing to do this, Polly. I know it's hard . . .**

(Poor Polly is found in appendix E.)

LEADER: **Thank you, Polly. Well, we are down to the last friend I'd like to introduce to you. Rad Rachael goes to school with Eileen, Sally, and Polly, and she actually** approached me to ask if she could share with you tonight. So . . . here's Rachael.

(Rad Rachael is found in appendix F.)

CHOOSE A SIDE

 Just before you choose a side (I know, there are four sides, which makes us a square), I want to go over one last part from *Secret Diary Unlocked* together. Let's look on page 97 *(School is out! Boy and it's about time)*. Follow along as I read . . . *(Read through page 100 [I was not freshwater, no matter how hard I tried to fool my teachers and my friends.])*

Those words from James chapter 3 need to help you with your decision tonight, girls. Your decision—I want to encourage you to make it based not only on the stories that were read to you, but also on this question: Have I, in the past week, used my tongue to both praise God and also to curse someone? If the answer to that is yes, then, ladies, you need to seriously consider aligning yourself with Mean Eileen or with Sidekick Sally. One of the greatest things we want to come to grips with tonight is the fact that you cannot come here and say you are person A, with the tongue that praises the Father and your welcoming hugs and smiles for everyone, but tomorrow head to school to become person B, with the tongue that curses your classmates and alienates other girls with your behavior.

So you have a decision to make now. You need to be bold . . . You need to be honest with yourself. The truth is, and you know it, that if you need to go to the Mean Eileen group, but you try to save face and go to the Rad Rachael group . . . everyone is going to know it, most of all yourself. It's okay to say tonight, "Oops, I've been trying to use my tongue for two different things, and that has GOT to stop." It's okay to make mistakes. It's okay to need correction. Proverbs 12:1 says, "Whoever loves discipline loves knowledge, but he who hates correction is stupid."

But most of all, everyone in this room right now needs to remember our rule about confidences . . . whatever happens in this room, stays in this room.

LAB: REVOLUTION

 **Now is the moment of truth, ladies.** *(Separate girls into four corners: Eileen's, Sally's, Polly's, and Rachael's.)* **Each group needs to take your copies of** *Secret Diary Unlocked* **and turn to the "My Struggle" section of chapter 6. Here you will find instructions to follow based on which corner you are aligned with right now. Each of you should count on also taking a few minutes to read chapter 7: "Revolution."** *(Have a mentor close each group in prayer after 10–15 minutes.)*

LESSON 6

MOM WAS RIGHT

A JOINT MOTHER/DAUGHTER SESSION

THE GOAL:

Girls and moms will attend session together to affirm their joint need for the mother/daughter bond to be nourished.

THINGS YOU'LL NEED:

- Tug-of-war rope
- Note cards for panel discussion
- Pens/pencils

GETTING READY:

- Read chapter 9 of *Secret Diary Unlocked*
- Preview study guide materials
- Have someone build mess pit for tug-of-war
- Prepare ten or more question cards

THE DEAL: TUG-OF-WAR

TIME: 15 MINUTES
THE POINT: GOOD OLD MESSY FUN! (AND MASSAGES!)
SUPPLIES: ROPE AND POSSIBLE MESS PIT

THE GAME: STORIES

TIME: 30 MINUTES
THE POINT: GIRLS AND MOMS SHARE MEANINGFUL STORIES
SUPPLIES: TEN(+) PREPARED QUESTION CARDS

THE DEAL: PANEL DISCUSSION

TIME: 20 MINUTES
THE POINT: GIRLS AND MOMS ANSWER NAGGING QUESTIONS
SUPPLIES: NOTE CARDS

THE DEAL: WRAP IT UP

TIME: 15 MINUTES
THE POINT: GIRLS AND MOMS WRITE LOVE NOTES
SUPPLIES: PRETTY NOTE PAPER; VARIETY OF BOXES
AND WRAPPING MATERIAL

This is designed to be a joint session for mothers/daughters,
though you may adapt it to remain girls only if you believe
that to be necessary with your group. Girls who do not have
mothers should bring a female relative, friend's mom, or a
mentor who plays the mother role in their life. Mother/daugh-
ter relationships are a little shaky for this age group and even
shakier for our culture in general. Some of your girls will not be
thrilled about the fact that their mothers will be attending this
session. That's okay. Do not let them dissuade you!

TUG-OF-WAR

You can choose between several ways of doing this event. You may choose clean tug-of-war, where two teams vie to pull one another over a designated line . . . or you can play messy tug-of-war! (Leave extra time for cleanup if you do this one.) The girls would love it if their mothers would agree just this once to get a little messy with them! Have a volunteer create a mud or Jello pit; play on two sides of a creek so the loser goes in. There is nothing quite so beneficial as making a memory together!

Say to the girls and moms: **Okay ladies, here begins the battle of moms and the teenage years! I know that you are occasionally warring at home, so we're giving you a safe place to settle things today. It's moms on one side of the rope and girls on the other! Losers give the winners a five-minute timed back or foot rub . . . winner's choice. So grab a spot on the rope and let's settle this thing once and for all! Ready, get set . . . Go!**

Be sure to follow through when all is said and done with the five-minute massage! (My prediction . . . moms will usually win!)

SESSION: STORIES

Each chapter of *Secret Diary Unlocked* that we have been through explores both Suzy's diary from 1979 as well as input from girls all over the United States. We usually begin our session reading excerpts from the book, but today, moms and daughters, you will write your own

chapter input. I am giving you each a note card with a question on top. Please answer the question with a short paragraph, but do not put your name on it.

Give each girl and each mother a note card. Here are five sample questions for each group. You may repeat questions or make up more of your own, depending on your group's size, but keep the questions positive.

QUESTIONS FOR GIRLS:

● Tell me a little bit about your relationship with your mom . . .

● What does your mom do that embarrasses you every time?

● Tell me one thing your mom does for you that you'd definitely like to do for your daughter someday . . .

● What is your favorite mom-ism? (That would be something like, "If you don't stop crying I'll give you something to cry about." Or, "You'll never know what I know and what I don't, so just tell the truth . . .")

● What's the one thing about your mom that you'd like to be able to manufacture and sell to other girls so they could have it, too?

QUESTIONS FOR MOMS:

● Tell me a little bit about your relationship with your daughter . . .

● What's your most striking memory of the day your daughter was born?

● What's the one thing about your daughter you'd like to be able to manufacture and sell to other moms so they could have it, too?

- When were you most proud of your little girl?

- What is the biggest lesson your daughter has taught you thus far?

Have the girls take turns reading Suzy's diary entries, and then you read cards from moms and daughters aloud. (You'll have to quickly proofread in advance, or have a co-leader do this for you so that there are no surprises that suddenly get read aloud. Though it would be a rare occurrence, it's good to be sure no negatives sneak in.) Ask the girls and moms: **Does Satan think it's worth his time to attack mother/daughter relationships? Why?**

PANEL DISCUSSION

We're going to have a panel discussion for our next session. I am going to give you note cards again, and this time I want each of you to write one question on your note card. If you are a mom, your question will begin with, "Why do girls . . ." If you are a girl, your question will begin, "Why do moms . . ."

The only rule here is that questions must not take an attacking or accusatory slant. It's okay to say, "Why do girls always minimize their computer screen when parents walk by?" but it should not say, "Why do you kids always feel like you have to sneak around and minimize your computer screen just because one of your parents is in the room with you?" Do you hear the difference between the two? We can ask good questions and get good answers without anyone having to feel

defensive. You may begin, and you have five minutes to come up with your one question . . .

Arrange moms and daughters in two lines or two horseshoes facing one another. You will be the mediator, reading one card at a time, first asking the girls a question and then asking a question of the mothers. Keep the tone light and fun, and encourage a lot of laughter. Again, tonight is about making some good memories.

WRAP IT UP

Read this section of *Secret Diary Unlocked* to the girls and moms. Be sure they are sitting next to one another for this last section.

> The longer I live and the more
> I watch my mom in action I am aware
> of the great Mom-Truth: No one
> on earth really loves me like my mom. She
> has told me that for years, but of course
> I thought it was just her pride talking.
> Turns out it's true. It's not a statement
> of quantity . . . It's not like Mom loves me
> THIIIIIIIIIIIIIIIS much and my husband loves
> me THIIIIIIIS much. They are different loves.
> Jonathan's always been friend, lover, and
> constant companion. He's my husband not only
> because he loves me, but also because he
> likes me. We chose each other, and we choose
> each other every single day.
>
> Mom's never had the luxury of choosing me!
> I grew inside of her, knit together in secret
> by God's design, and she had to be surprised
> by me like the rest of the world. She was able

to shape and form me a great deal, but she could only work with the material that she was given. I am an introvert, an athlete, an animal lover, competitive, sometimes shy, sometimes sarcastic . . . Jonathan chose that. Mom was stuck with it . . . and yes, maybe helped develop it all a bit. And yet Mom loves me. She loves me with the fiercest of jealousies. God help the person who tries to mess with Mama's little girl, because my sweet little hundred-pound, 5'2" mother will become a force to reckon with. She is my biggest fan, my defender, and truest girl confidante. I pray that my beautiful daughters know that I strive to be nothing less for them . . . minus the hundred-pound part. I think that goal is long out of reach.

Now it's time to wrap it up. You have one last piece of paper in front of you. I want you to write on this paper a short note to your mother or to your daughter. Then I want you to place it in one of the boxes you see on the wrapping table, and I want you to beautifully wrap this gift of love. There are a lot of decorating tools for your use on the table. This gift is to be given to whomever you have written the note to at some point tomorrow. Maybe you will place it on a pillow, maybe you will put it at a place setting, leave it on a car seat, have it delivered during school . . . Increase the blessing by adding the element of surprise! Before you leave tonight, give each other a great big hug and pray for each other. And have fun with your gift giving tomorrow!!!

LESSON 7

BAD GIRL WANNABE

THE GOAL:

Girls will identify areas of rebellion in their lives and ask God to lead them instead to another place.

THINGS YOU'LL NEED:

- GHOST worksheet (appendix G)
- Pens/pencils

GETTING READY:

- Read chapter 8 of *Secret Diary Unlocked*
- Preview study guide materials
- Use a small team to create "Wall of Normal"

THE DEAL: WALL OF NORMAL

TIME: 15 MINUTES
THE POINT: "NORMAL" AND "GOOD" ARE NOT SAME
SUPPLIES: CONSTRUCTED ART WALL

THE GAME: GHOST

TIME: 30 MINUTES
THE POINT: FIVE RULES FOR EXITING REBELLION
SUPPLIES: GHOST WORKSHEET

THE DEAL: PRAYER HUDDLES

TIME: 10 MINUTES
THE POINT: PRAYER REQUESTS FOR SELF/OTHERS
SUPPLIES: NONE

Psychologists will tell you that rebellion is not only normal for teenagers, but it is something therapists desire to see in order for proper development. As adults, this is a hard theory to embrace. Don't worry—it's not entirely a biblical principle! In this lesson the girls will have to wrestle with some basic word definitions. If something is "normal," is it necessarily "good"? If something is "helpful," is it also "good"? These are slightly abstract concepts for young girls, but important ones to grab hold of, and the younger the better. By telling your story, and my story, of victory over rebellion, we can give the girls confidence that they are normal . . . and that's good . . . but we can also call them to excellence!

THE WALL OF NORMAL

Select a wall in your meeting area to dub the "Wall of Normal." Hang along the wall, art-gallery style, about twenty pictures of things that are perfectly "normal" in their proper setting, but would not be even remotely "normal" in the girls' worlds.

Examples might be an African native who has a HUGE hoop through her lip or ear, "normal" fashions from the Far East, a photo of a canine that is a polydactyl (having two or three extra toes on its back legs . . . completely normal for large mountain breeds such as the mastiff), a regional dish such as chitlins that your girls have never encountered, headlines from a celebrity breakup, a funny newborn baby picture (sometimes they look kind of, well . . . weird). You get the picture. I actually Googled "normal things that look weird" and got some good ideas there. Get a team of two or three creative people to help you and you can pull this off quite well.

When the girls come in, simply explain to them that these are photos of "normal" things . . . Put a banner across the display that says something like, "Normal can sometimes be hard on others" or "Do you want to be normal?" Just allow this to be a fun browsing time as girls arrive.

SESSION: GHOST

Bring it in, girls! Okay. We just had some fun looking at totally bizarre photos, but did you catch on to what it is they all have in common? They are all things that are normal, but don't necessarily evoke good

feelings or warm feelings for the one who sees them. Why did I torture you with them? To illustrate that there is something in YOUR life . . . and mine . . . that is normal but not always pleasant. It's REBELLION.

Chapter 8 of Secret Diary Unlocked deals largely with the idea that rebellion is "normal." Let's check out the diary sections. *Have the girls take turns reading Suzy's diary entries and responses from other girls aloud.* <u>Ask the girls:</u> **Why do you think rebellion, in general, freaks out most adults? Have you freaked out over rebellion in a friend's or a sibling's life? Tell us about that.**

I guess we'd all be in agreement that rebellion is normal for most teenagers, at least to some degree. There have even been kids who use church as a means to rebel against parents. The parents are adamantly against Christianity or organized religion . . . so the girl sneaks behind their backs to attend a youth group. The spirit behind it is all the same. I am going to do what I want to do. Or as three-year-olds say, "You're not the boss of me."

This isn't a lecture. I have a story just like many of you . . . (Share your story of teenage rebellion. Be careful not to share details that will put any vivid pictures of sin in the girls' minds . . . consider how I told my story of rebellion in chapter 8. I could easily have left some nasty images in their little minds! Tell as much of the story as you can in as general of terms as you can. Be sure it is Jesus' rescue of you that receives glory and not your rebellious attitude.)

I know some of your stories, and others I don't know, but no matter the situation, there's really no way to address the issue of rebellion other than to ask what does God want us to do about it? Psychologists will tell you teen re-bellion is normal. I won't necessarily argue. Your parents

may be reactive rather than compassionate. That's not a good response, but it is probably as normal as your own rebellion. But ask yourself what God says, because that's the only place it's safe to point our compass.

First of all, what's a Bible study without one really good acronym? Here's ours: GHOST. That's glorify, humble, obey, submit, and turn. It will give us a good picture of where God needs us to be even though we are beginning a fight for our independence.

 Glorify—can you think of any way that GLORIFY could be part of exiting rebellion? *(Allow girls to think aloud.)* How about this? God says that everything we do, whether we eat or drink, should all be done to his glory (1 Corinthians 10:31. God gives us just a ton of freedom in our lives. Paul told the church at Corinth that everything was permissible . . . it's just that not everything is beneficial. So while it might be perfectly okay with Amy's mom and with the theater owner that you be sold a ticket for an R-rated movie, that is a bad compass reading for you to rely on. God's Word is first . . . does that movie please Him or grieve Him? And Mom and Dad are second . . . Honor your mother and father. It's already hard, isn't it? You may have a hard time discerning whether God would find the movie appropriate, and you may flat out disagree with your parents. But glorifying God is not about doing only the things that we agree with. It's about saying, "Man, I just don't see it, but okay . . . I'll lay it down. I give up." Think about Abraham being asked to place Isaac on the altar. Do you think there is ANY way on earth that God's request to sacrifice his own son lined up with what Abraham wanted?

H is going to represent Humble, as in "Humble yourselves in the sight of the Lord." The most common definition of humble is probably to be the opposite of boastful. Don't brag. Don't think too highly of yourself. But there is another definition we're going to use here . . . any guesses? *(Allow girls time to think aloud.)* When we say humble in this case, we're going to be talking about taking the back seat instead of the front seat. Do you ever fight with your brothers or sisters over who gets to sit in the front? Actually we all fight for the front seat every day. We want the most respect, the most attention, the best stuff . . . and we want to get our own way. This is part of what rebellion is made of. It's like those birds in Finding Nemo: Mine. Mine. Mine. Mine. If we are going to follow the model we have been creating so far, then we have a really old station wagon here . . . God's in the front seat, Mom and Dad come next, and then we're in that seat all the way in the back that faces the other way! *"Do nothing out of selfish ambition or vain conceit, but in humility, consider others better than yourselves. Each of you should look not only to your own interests, but also to the interests of others"(Philippians 2:3–4).* It's like Thanksgiving dinner where the kids always have to sit at the little table off to the side. That's where God wants us to volunteer to sit . . .

 The O is Obey. There's a little trick to obedience, though. This is because every child— all of your friends, regardless of their background story—every child knows she should obey her parents, the law, teachers, etc. The key word there is "should." So it's not enough to just agree that what has been asked of us is good. The one who does what has been asked . . . she is the one who has obeyed, right? Jesus tells a story in the book of Matthew to a bunch of Pharisees who are questioning His authority—He wants them to see that though they sneer at the tax collectors and the prostitutes (the rebels of the community) many of these once rebellious people are actually being welcomed into the Kingdom of God, while the Pharisees . . . well, they don't stand much of a chance. Let's read Matthew 21:28–32 together. *(Read parable and have girls follow along in their own Bibles.)* This part of our study doesn't address our attitude—it addresses what we DO. It really doesn't matter how compliant and sweet we seem on the outside; it doesn't matter if we have all of the adults around us fooled by our pleasant demeanor. Proverbs says, "Even a child is known by his actions, by whether his conduct is right and pure"(20:11). In the end, it is about what we do, not how sweet and innocent we seem on the outside.

 The S in our acronym stands for Submit. On a scale of one to ten, how stubborn are you? *(Allow girls time to enjoy their answers.)* We can be a pretty "stiff-necked people," as God likes to sometimes call us in Scripture. Are you familiar with the term "Crying Uncle"? This originated all the way back in the Roman Empire. When Roman children were set upon by a bully, or even during a friendly wrestling match, they would need to say, "Patrue, mi Patruissimo," or "Uncle, my best Uncle," in order to be released. Today we still use the term when someone is perhaps wrestling with us or tickling us and we decide we are ready to BEG them to stop! It might be this kind of scenario when you "wrestle" with your parents—they may hold you down until you have to cry uncle, but with God I'll warn you it's a little different. Rather than pin us down or force us into submission, God kind of just lets us go. He turns us over to our own will and our own devices, and he knows how it will end up for us. He knows that pregnancy, a DUI, the loss of a friend over betrayed confidences, groundings, guilt, and shame all might await us at the end of our rebellion. While He has the ability—and every right—to strong-arm us, he chooses to let our submission be a response to His kindness instead. It is God's kindness that leads us to repentance (Romans 2:4). We go astray, we pay the price, but in the end we find no condemnation from him. He just says, "You ready to try this again? How about trying it My way this time?" And I think you'll find that in the end, most parents are much the same . . .

 Our final letter, T, is for Turn. The idea behind repentance is that you would do a 180 degree turn. Think about it. 360 degrees is a circle, so what would 180 be? (*Have a couple of girls who think they get it stand and do a 180 for you*). That's right. The linear picture of a 180 would be to walk the other way. As we begin to work out our issues with rebellion, learning to assert independence without sinning against God or our parents, it's important to know that while individual victories are great our overall direction of travel might need a complete overhaul. There is a great football story from the year 1929—a great story whether you like football or not. It was the Rose Bowl and California was playing Georgia Tech. There was no score in the game yet when a Georgia Tech player fumbled the ball. A California defensive player by the name of Roy Regal picked up the fumble and was only about 30 yards from a touchdown when he was hit by a Georgia Tech player, causing him to become disoriented. Somehow he was now running the WRONG WAY down the field. He ran for 60 yards before one of his own players managed to stop him and turn him around. "You're running the wrong way!" his teammate shouted. But it was too late. The Georgia Tech players had caught up to Regal as well, and they tackled him, pushing him back to his own one-yard line. Worse yet, his team went on to lose the game. His nickname for the rest of his life? Wrong Way Roy Regal.[2]

Regal's not so unusual. God forbid we should go through life with no one loving us enough to chase us down and tell us we are going the wrong way! Everyone needs that chase now and then. Your pastor has to make U-turns, your parents, every man or woman you've ever read about in the Bible. U-turn city! The question is . . . will you be wise enough to turn around when someone catches up to you? Proverbs 13:13 says, "He who scorns instruction will pay for it, but he who respects a command is rewarded."

PRAYER HUDDLES

Provide two prayer huddle choices for the girls, each one "staffed" by adult leaders. One huddle should be for girls who want to request prayer for themselves. Perhaps they realize after completing their GHOST sheet that they have a lot of work to do in the area of turning from rebellion. Most of your leaders should be present at this huddle so that individualized prayer can take place. Brief these adults in advance that they need to be available for any girl they pray with even after this session. It may be necessary to go to the girl's parents together or she may need additional support if her commitment to turn means she is going to step away from a group of friends. It takes a while for iron to sharpen iron . . . so these ladies need to be available.

The second huddle can be for girls who want to put in some serious intercession time for friends/relatives/maybe even parents who are in rebellion. This can be done as a larger group if only one adult is available, but if there are more leaders available it would be good to break this group into smaller parts as well. Be sure these girls know that they need to be the one *chasing* Wrong Way Roy down the field—their prayers should be accompanied by that actual chase!

LESSON 8

GLAD I'M A GIRL

THE GOAL:

Girls will hand over to God any bitterness and envy they have had toward people who have received more glory than they have . . . it's not so much about envying boys as it is envy in general!

THINGS YOU'LL NEED:

- Pre-selected DVDs for viewing; write cues in advance
- Three to five (or more if possible) visitors to lead service projects

GETTING READY:

- Read chapter 10 of *Secret Diary Unlocked*
- Preview Study Guide materials
- Photocopy appendix H—One for each girl and leader
- Invite three to five women from the community to lead small groups of girls in unseen, unsung service projects
- Arrange for any needed transportation and possible different pick-up locations

THE GAME: WORSHIP STUDY

TIME: 20 MINUTES
~~THE RULES: COMPARE TWO TYPES OF WORSHIP~~
PARTY SUPPLIES: TWO PRE-SELECTED DVDS

THE GAME: MY DESIRE, MY FEAR

TIME: 20 MINUTES
THE RULES: A PRAYER ABOUT RECOGNITION
PARTY SUPPLIES: COPIES OF POEM FROM APPENDIX H

THE GAME: SERVING WITH THE BIG DOGS

TIME: 40 MINUTES
~~THE RULES: WALKING THE TALK—SERVICE WITH NO PRAISE!~~
PARTY SUPPLIES: PREARRANGED SERVICE JOBS

This was an extremely difficult chapter for me. I was torn between two possibilities. Either this chapter was not meant to be in the book, or it needed to be in the book more so than others. I knew there was no in-between on this one. It seemed to me at first this was simply about gender jealousy—I know I was often jealous of boys and this sentiment made regular appearances in my diaries. However, as I began to work through these issues I began to see that it was as simple as this: All my life I have craved attention, respect, and recognition, and it was my belief that boys receive these things in significantly greater measure than girls. This may or may not be true as a generality, but the greater truth is that while we were created male and female, the reception of glory was meant for neither gender.

WORSHIP STUDY

What are some of your thoughts on worship music in the church? What is the best worship experience, musically, that you have ever had? Would you agree or disagree with this statement: People were built for worship, and

everyone worships something. *(Allow girls time to answer each question.)*

We are going to take a look at two video clips tonight. Both show people involved in acts of worship. The first is from _____. *(This first clip should be of a contemporary worship event such as Passion's "One Day" or perhaps a Chris Tomlin, David Crowder, or Delirious concert. These can be found on Amazon.com. It is possible there are movies such as Will Smith's* Pursuit of Happyness *that will suffice.)*

Now let's take a look at this clip from _____. *(This second clip will be of idolatry, perhaps something like Beatlemania. There are many such DVDs in the music section of your local rental place. You may also show a clip from* That Thing You Do, *which portrays a mania similar to that of the Beatles movie.)*

What differences do you see between the two clips that we observed?

Have you ever personally experienced anything like the first DVD clip we watched?

Have you ever been guilty of "worshiping" in the same manner as shown in the second clip?

Have you ever imagined being on the receiving end of this type of adoration?

MY DESIRE, MY FEAR

Give the girls a copy of Mother Teresa's poem, found in appendix F. Have the girls gather in a circle and explain that during this next section, they will be participating in what is called a "peace candle." Turn the lights down low in the room and light one large, fragrant candle.
The candle provides ambiance, but also signifies that serious

words are being spoken, and only the person who possesses the candle may speak. Explain this rule to the girls.

<u>Say</u>: **This poem, believe it or not, was written by Mother Teresa.[1] She and the sisters who served in anonymity with her on the streets of Calcutta, India prayed these words daily as they went about the tireless task of serving a city so poor they could not save it, so dirty and diseased they could never clean it, and so wretched in spirit it could never pay them back.**

Read the poem aloud to the girls.

<u>Say</u>: **Now we will send the peace candle around the circle. When you receive it, share the answer to two questions with the group: Which of the lines in the poem above represents your greatest desire? Which one represents your greatest fear?**

(Be sure you are participating in this discussion as well. Share your fear and your desire. Be vulnerable so the girls have a chance to see that you have not yet arrived.)

SERVING WITH THE BIG DOGS

 Introduce your visitors to the girls. This should be a group of three to five women from your church who are notoriously servant-minded, quiet in spirit (not loud, up-front women, though the church needs such women as well), and who serve a somewhat overlooked but vital need in the church or community. In my church, for example, there is a woman who is passionate about missions and missionary kids. She writes them letters, sends gifts, and keeps the supply of missionary conference costumes and decorations in order. She must communicate via e-mail and letter with over fifty mission-

aries! There is also a woman who started a ministry to serve Haitians by cooperating with a single female missionary who lives and works in Haiti. She frequently holds fund-raisers and sends large packages of everyday necessities to her Haitian friends. She met two Haitian guys on a cruise ship who said they wanted to study in the United States. Guess what? They now share a basement apartment in her house and attend school here in town! These women are the big dogs—doing what God says a woman of noble character should do!

Perhaps in your church there are women who like to send cards of encouragement to struggling families. Maybe there is the proverbial cookie ministry lady, or the woman who likes to visit shut-ins. A woman who cleans others' homes just to bless them . . . the one who painstakingly maintains the church library . . . someone who babysits and doesn't charge for it . . . There are all kinds of unsung heroes in our churches, never desiring the recognition, never seeking approval, unafraid of seeming insignificant.

Divide your girls into groups—one group for every visitor. Send them out to do a service project that will not be likely to garner any respect, notice, or recognition. They will not report back to the group, receive a certificate or thank you note . . . whatever service they perform this day may go completely unnoticed.

But pray with the girls as they go out—pray that they will be like the woman of noble character who brings honor and glory to God, who is blessed by the work God prepares for her to do, and who does not need to be recognized, coddled, mentioned, noticed, or emulated. It is enough to know that God is tickled silly pink . . . madly in love with her!

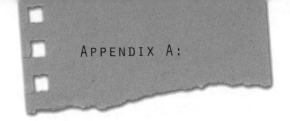

TRUTH

- If you had $100 that had to be spent totally selfishly, what would you buy?

- When is the last time you told a lie and what was it?

- Tell about a time you were mean to someone. Did you regret it?

- What do you really watch on television when no one is home?

- What do you pretend to like doing with friends, but you secretly hate?

- Tell the group the absolutely coolest thing about your parental units . . .

- True or false—when no one is looking I drink milk right out of the container.

- I'd eat more if out with my friends than if out on a date.

- What toys do you still play with . . . but only when no one else is around?

- My biggest fear about school is . . .

- On a scale of 1 to 10, how much effort do you put into your chores at home?

- True or false—I usually hide my IM windows when someone walks up behind me.

- What would be the most effective punishment you could receive from your parents?

- Would you turn in a best friend for cheating on a test? Would you tell your mom?

- Which are you—an eye-roller or a tongue-sticker-outer?

- Have you ever pretended to not know the answer in class? Why?

- What is one career dream you have that you've told very few people?

- T/F When people say, "I don't pay attention to song lyrics" they are lying. How about you???

- Tell about a time when you told your parents you were going somewhere other than where you really went.

- What was your worst day ever and what made it that way?

- What is the ugliest item of clothing in your wardrobe? Do you wear it?

- We all have a biggest secret. Instead of telling what your biggest secret is, instead, truthfully explain WHY you keep this thing a secret.

- If you could live in any book or movie, what would it be and why? Would you be yourself or one of the characters?

DARE

- Run around the room making monkey noises for 15 seconds. Add 5 seconds for every time you stop making noise!

- Cup your hands together as tight as you can, then fill them with water. Now sit down and hold your hands over your legs. You must try and keep any water from leaking or spilling for an entire round.

- Give the group your biggest, loudest belch that you can bring up . . . but try not to bring anything up!

- Have someone hold your nose and cover your mouth. Now scream as loud as you can.

- Every party needs party hats. The person who goes next gets to find you "something" to wear on your head. Whatever they give you, you must wear for the rest of the game.

- Do your best impression of a puppy for a minimum of one minute. You can stop when the group feels that you have done a convincing job.

- Go to the nearest fridge. Choose another group member to: Pick whatever is in the upper left corner, closest to the front. Have her mix it with whatever is in the lower right corner, closest to the back. Now you choose one thing from the door and have her mix it in as well. Take a BIG mouthful of the concoction and swallow it!

- You get to take a nice, cold shower with your clothes on! Take off your shoes and socks, then stand in a shower and turn on the cold water for 5 seconds. You MUST STAND UNDER the water.

- Eat your favorite food. Before you swallow it, spit it out, and re-eat it.

- Put on a music channel with a video of a band/artist doing a dance routine. You now have to copy it (and exaggerate) for
30 seconds. If no one can find a music video playing, you lucked out.

- Stand on your left foot, for 2 minutes. Every time you fall, the time starts over again. No one may touch you, but they can try to make you laugh. (Better put a time limit on this one!)

- The next five people in the group, going in order of turns, may add one word to the following sentence: For the next three rounds you must _____. After the group has each added their word, you must perform the dare.

- Stick a finger in your mouth, at least to the first knuckle. Leave it there until the next turn.

Hey girls! I'm really excited that you are going through this study with a group of your friends. While I write this study guide and book I find myself wrestling with whether or not I envy you. I mean, I like a lot of things about my life currently, such as being a mom, my three pets (I don't think my mom would have ever let me have three pets at once—she still says I'm crazy), having financial freedom, the fact that I'm in Florida right now and can hear the ocean rolling in behind me . . .

Yet I feel a little envious about the fact that you are in your golden years of friendship right now. Trust me; it doesn't get much better than high school and college where friends are concerned. As I think about it, I miss the freedom to crash at someone else's house. Do you know how long it's been since my friends and I have felt the release to go absolutely berserk in public? (We're all dignified now, you know.) I can't remember the last time I called a friend and said, "What are you doing?" only to hear her say, "Nothing, how about you?" to which I could then say, "Nothing. You wanna do something?" to which she would say, "I guess," and suddenly I have something to do . . . I never have nothing to do (think about it; that's not a double negative!)

So . . . it's that envy I want to take a look at in this lesson. I really do believe that most of our meltdowns with friends revolve around the fact that we're feeling jealous of someone or something. They have something that we want, we don't like the fact that we don't have it, and the next thing you know something we regret is flying out of our mouths. You know what I mean. It just seems girl-friendships are filled with regret.

We're going to go through three steps now that you can take to protect those precious friendships—and trust me, these will apply throughout life to your husband, your children, your co-workers. For you see, these are steps that make you a good friend, not steps that will necessarily change anyone else. Are you ready?

Step One:

Think about _____ before I think about _____.

This week I will _____

Step Two:

Tell someone you _____ that you are struggling with jealousy.

I will talk to _____ this week about how I've been feeling.

Step Three:

Do a _____ of _____ for someone you _____ today.

I am going to _____
for _____.

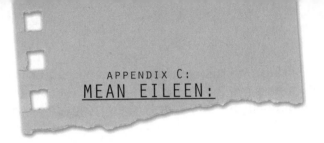

Hi. My name is Eileen and I'm totally sure you know who I am. Most people in the school do know me. I run with all the popular kids and I date all the hottest guys. We're not a clique or anything. Anyone else is totally welcome to join us. I'm serious. I mean, I guess there are *some* rules for joining. There are certain people you probably shouldn't talk to anymore if you hang out with us. And there is kind of this dress code to be maintained. It's not written or anything, but you'd catch on soon enough. But you can't wear the same things as me. You have to still be individual.

I've been thinking a lot lately about things at school—they're not so good. I mean, it was pretty cool at first to have a lot of girls follow me and seem to want to do whatever I was doing, but then it just got annoying. I felt like they were trying to become me and no one was just themselves any more. That's why I say you have to be an individual. I'm kind of sick of all the posers, even though I guess it's a little flattering.

The truth is, I don't really know what to do with all the flattery. Girls are always telling me how awesome I look and imitating the things I say . . . it's like I'm famous or something, but I know that I'm really not. I don't even think I'm that pretty to tell you the truth. I mean, sometimes I do. But a lot of the time when I look in the mirror I just see all the things that are wrong with me. (*Threaten your listeners a little . . .*) You'd better not tell anyone that!

I don't know what to do. I think I might like to have a little of the attention taken off of me, but I'm also afraid of what might happen if I'm not the leader anymore. Will the guys still like me? If I back down just a little, the girls who are imitating me right now—will they try to take power and start treating me like I'm not as good as them?—'cause I don't trust them at all. I know they'd like to be me, but what they don't know is that it's not really all that great being me.

And another thing—I've been feeling kind of bad about some things I've said to—or about—other girls. I don't think I really meant them, they just came out. See, I go to church and everything, but it's so hard at school. I feel mad a lot of the time, and I don't even know why. So I guess maybe I've been taking it out on some of the girls who aren't so . . . popular? I don't know. I just think I shouldn't have said some of what I've said . . . like about Sally's friend . . .

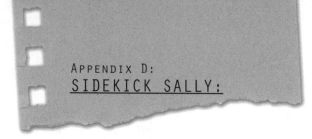

Hi, um, like ___(leader's name)_____ said, my name is Sally. This is kind of scary being up in front of a lot of people, 'cause I'm kind of more used to having my friends with me. Okay— um, I mostly run around with Eileen and her friends. Or I am one of her friends . . . I guess.

Actually, a lot of us are really confused about Eileen. At first she seemed really cool—and she *is* I guess— but I don't know. It's definitely true that good things happen to me when I'm with this group. Like, I get to go to dances with the best guys and all of the popular people know my name. I sit at the best lunch table, and I can see other girls turn their heads when we walk by in the hallway. And that feels kind of good, you know? Like I matter around here.

But something pretty bad happened last week and now I feel totally confused about what to do. Okay, there's this girl who I used to be really good friends with for like the past ten years. We've hung out a ton since we were about four years old. She lived across the street from me . . . well, she still does, I guess. Anyhow, I noticed that once this school year started she was treating me differently in the halls. My mom would ask all the time why she never came over anymore and I was like, "I don't know. She never talks to me at school."

Last weekend I saw her at a party and I was like, "Hey, I haven't see you all year!" And then I was kind of blown away because she said that Eileen and a couple of my other friends have been calling her really bad names and IM-ing her and saying things like she'd better stay away from me and that I was telling them really bad things about her . . . and none of it's true! And the worst part about the whole thing is that she didn't believe me. I think she wanted to, but I could see in her face that she didn't, and I'm trying to figure out how this happened because she was like my best friend!

I don't know why Eileen and the others don't like her, 'cause she's really nice, and she's smart, too. Her dad is a doctor and she totally wants to be one some day. So anyhow, I asked Eileen about it at school and she just laughed—and then of course all the other girls laughed, too, even though some of them didn't even know what was going on. When Eileen laughs, it's best if you just go along. Eileen said it was basically all true and that she just couldn't afford for someone like Polly (that's my friend) to be hanging all over us. "She's not exactly a good luck charm," Eileen said. Whatever.

So I guess I have to figure out what to do. I don't want to lose Eileen as a friend, I really don't, but I'm beginning to think it might be more because I'm afraid of her than anything else. And I'm afraid that she can see to it that I have NO friends .

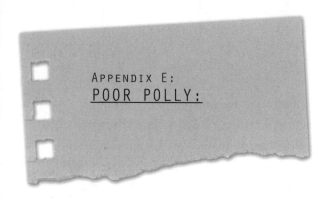

Hi. My name is Polly. *(To leader)* What am I supposed to say?

LEADER: **Just tell them what happened.**

POLLY: *(Not looking happy about doing this . . .)* Well, I pretty much hate school this year. It's ugh! Okay, it started out okay—I don't have a lot of friends, but my best friend for, like, forever was going to be there with me, so I figured it would be fine. Plus, I'm taking all AP classes and hopefully one class at community college this spring, so I have to focus a lot on academics anyhow.

So the first few weeks are fine—Sally and I walk to school together every day, say good-bye in the hallway (we don't have any classes together and her locker is practically over in Malaysia), and then we'd sometimes end up walking home together, too. I guess I was noticing that we didn't have a lot in common to talk about anymore . . . and the other thing that was bugging me is that she was talking really negatively about some girls that we had always kind of been friends with. But I guess I didn't give it too much thought.

I noticed she was dressing differently, too. She used to wear a lot of jeans and sweatshirts, sweaters—pretty basic stuff. But now she's wearing all this makeup and jewelry, and these really tight, short skirts . . . She never wore skirts before. One morning it was kind of cold and she was wearing flippin' shorts and a belly shirt! She was freezing, but it was like she *had* to wear it or something. It was weird.

So, it was like overnight that she quit walking to school with me. One morning I stood on the sidewalk and waited for at least 15 minutes before her mom came out and told me she had left almost an hour earlier with Mean Eileen. I couldn't believe it! Sally with Eileen? She's like the most popular girl in the school! She hasn't waited for me in the mornings since.

That was right about when I started getting the notes in my locker and the nasty IMs on my computer. I won't tell you what they said because I actually don't use that kind of language, but it is pretty bad! It doesn't really happen any-more—I guess they think they have me in my place and all now, but for a while it was just about killing me. They said I did things with guys that were flat out lies. They told people not to hang out with me or even sit with me. They jammed nasty stuff up the air slots in my locker. They wrote about me on the bathroom stalls. They'd call my house and hang up. And I have NO idea why they did any of it, other than Sally was my friend.

My mom is like, "Polly, there has to be some reason." But there isn't. There really isn't. And I'm totally confused about Sally. She insists that she has nothing to do with it, but it's not like she invited me to meet her tomorrow morning or stood up for me or anything. All I know is that school stinks and I can't wait to get out of there. I feel sick.

Thank you, _____ (*Leader's Name*). Yeah, I actually asked if I could come talk to you all because I'm really bothered by something I've seen happening at my school here lately. I'm a senior this year, which is cool. Big man on campus and all . . . minus the man part.

So anyhow, I've been watching this drama thing unfold all year . . . this story you've been hearing about. I'm kind of one of those people who doesn't really have a "group"—I pretty much like everybody and I think everybody likes me. So I've been around to hear Eileen and Sally's friends trashing Polly. It's been really nasty sometimes. And I need to speak up first for Eileen. I've seen her face after a few of these attacks, and I can tell it's true that she's really torn about what she's done. She's one of the coolest people I know when you can get her to yourself. I don't understand why she's so different around other people. But yeah, that bugged me watching all that.

At first I didn't get Sally, either. She's an amazing girl, too—smart, funny. But when she's around Eileen it's like she turns into this little robot that can't think or speak for herself. I know Sally, and this is *NOT* her! She's never been mean to Polly, not even once. But I've seen her do some of these things to other girls. I've seen her whisper when girls walk by and then laugh—

oh man, that drives you nuts when people do that to you, doesn't it? I've seen her stick things in people's lockers and then run away laughing. She's done all the things that people have done to Polly—it's just that she's done it to Kim, Darla, and Jenny. You get what I mean. I guess she's just kind of protected Polly because of their past, but she's in it all the same.

But here's the crazy thing that happened. I was watching all of this for several weeks and getting really mad at Eileen and Sally and all of the other girls. My friends—I can't really explain who I hang with at lunch, we're such an eclectic group, but mostly kids from my youth group—my friends and I were watching Polly sitting alone at lunch and talking about how much it ticked us off that girls were doing that to her . . . All of a sudden it hit me like a brick. I'm watching this happen, but what am I doing about it? Have I ever stood up to Eileen? No. Have I ever once invited poor Polly to sit with us? No—I've just watched her from across the room like she was the poor leper child or something.

So I decided to do something about it. I grabbed my friend Ashley from the lunch table and I said, "Let's go, baby." And we marched right over to Polly and sat down with her . . . she's spending the night with us on Friday. Yep, yep. Turns out she's pretty cool. Here's the thing though. If God hadn't pretty much hit me upside the head, I might have let this Polly thing go. And I hate to think that Polly could still be sitting all alone . . . or that I could have missed out on, potentially, a really good friend.

GHOST:

G : _____

Glorifying God is not about doing only the things we _____ with.

One thing I've been asked to do that I don't really want to do is . . .

H : _____

When we say humble in this case, we're going to be talking about taking the _____ _____ instead of the _____ _____.

What's the worst thing that can happen if I actually don't get my own way?

O : _____

In the end, it is about what we _____, not about how _____ and _____ we seem on the outside.

What have I said I would do that I haven't done yet?

I will obey and do it on _____!

_____

While He has the _____—and every right—to _____ us, He chooses to let our submission be a response to His _____ instead.

Uncle! My best Uncle! I need to surrender . . .

_____

While individual _____ are great our overall _____ of travel might need a complete _____.

Who has been trying to catch up to me lately?

Have they caught me? Why or why not?

I'm going to do a 180 from . . .

APPENDIX H:

Deliver me, O Jesus,
From the desire of being loved,
From the desire of being extolled,
From the desire to being honored,
From the desire of being praised,
From the desire of being preferred,
From the desire of being consulted,
From the desire of being approved,
From the desire of being popular,
From the fear of being humiliated,
From the fear of being despised,
From the fear of suffering rebukes,
From the fear of being calumniated*,
From the fear of being forgotten,
From the fear of being wronged,
From the fear of being ridiculed,
From the fear of being suspected.
Amen.

*lied about

CHAPTER NOTES

BOY CRAZY:

1. Harry F. Harlow, "Love in Infant Monkeys;" (http://darkwing.uoregon.edu/~adoption/archive/HarlowLIM.htm), 1959.

GIRLFRIENDS:

1.The Barna Group, http://www.barna.org

REBELLION:

1. (http://www.word-detective.com/back-y.html)

2. Dr. Ronald W. Scates, "Tear Away Jerseys and Other Acts of Repentence" (Baltimore, MD: Central Presbyterian Church, 1999.) www.centralpc.org

GLAD I'M A GIRL

1. (http://home.comcast.net/~motherteresasite/prayers.html)